How Many Lemons Are There?

Seed Learning

How many lemons are there?

There are four.

There are
four lemons.

How many mangoes are there?

There are five.

There are
five mangoes.

How many pineapples are there?

There are six.

There are
six pineapples.

How many cherries are there?

There are seven.

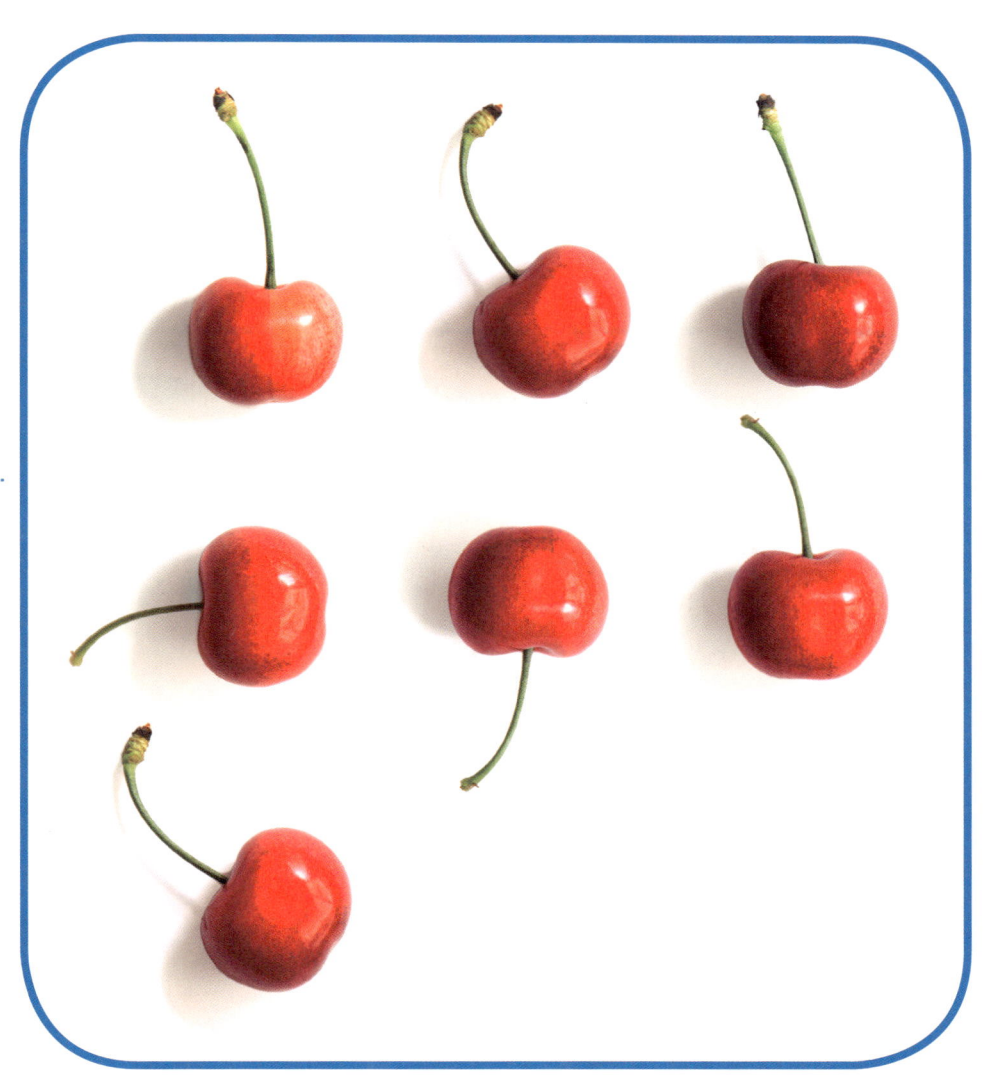

There are
seven cherries.

How many pears are there?

There are eight.

There are
eight pears.

How many plums are there?

There are nine.

There are
nine plums.

How many blueberries are there?

There are ten.

There are
ten blueberries.

Let's learn about Obon.

August

Sunday	Monday	Tuesday	Wednesday	Thursday	Friday	Saturday
						1
2	3	4	5	6	7	8
9	10	11	12	(13)	14	15
16	17	18	19	20	21	22
23	24	25	26	27	28	29
30	31					

Trace the word August
and circle the date.